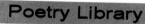

Vinland

VINLAND

Jamie Ross

FOUR WAY BOOKS
TRIBECA

Please direct all inquiries to:
Editorial Office
Four Way Books
POB 535, Village Station
New York, NY 10014
www.fourwaybooks.com

Library of Congress Cataloging-in-Publication Data

Ross, Jamie, 1946-
Vinland : poems / Jamie Ross.
p. cm.
"Winner of the Four Way Books Intro Prize."
ISBN 978-1-935536-99-4 (pbk.)
I. Title.
PS3618.O84527V56 2010
811'.6--dc22

2009029461

This book is manufactured in the United States of America
and printed on acid-free paper.

Four Way Books is a not-for-profit literary press.
We are grateful for the assistance we receive
from individual donors, public arts agencies, and private foundations.

This publication is made possible with public funds
from the National Endowment for the Arts.

Distributed by University Press of New England
One Court Street, Lebanon, NH 03766

We are a proud member of
the Council of Literary Magazines and Presses.

Funding for this book was provided in part by a generous donation in memory of John J. Wilson.

NATIONAL
ENDOWMENT
FOR THE ARTS
A great nation
deserves great art

[clmp]

Contents

For the New World

I Open His Book

Still he climbs, with his pack
and sample sacks, sandstone scree
crumbling from the cliffs, the
uplift ocean beds that stream
above Nevada, crest the Bighorn Range,
blanket the Wind Rivers. How

my father sings
with his hammer against rock, peen-ball
clean, steel chisels ringing
as he clears each face away. How
the fish swim as he sets them free, fossils
in this ocean that he cleaves and charts,

ancients in this story he encompasses
and enters. They course
within his fascia, histories of water
welling in each bone, the crust tectonics
that a family can drop. That a weight
can disperse. As leaves spread in autumn

on a New England farm, when night
comes down granite, and the mounting
northern glaciers spill across their zones.
As a man might spread, reading to his son,
· before lights go dim, candles extinguished,
the bedcovers re-drawn. How young

my father looks in his helplessness, tilted
on the pillow, his ribs wrapped in layers, pierced
by tubes. How the great seas of China
move their flow in him, the pull of the moon
through all its tidal vaults, the call
of those who cruise the vast crossing lakes

where he spends his new adventure, one
breath rising, the next
diving deep.

Moving Sheep Across a Road

the bridges white tortillas flocked with brown
a thousand here the oven with its stones the surface

over over. Turn us in this season, of the tiny
red, the pepper trees, a shepherd's dream

it walks. Because the snow is late again the

fire the instant flowers the thousand violet
asters east-west north from Mexico, Juliana

in her necklace and salt-cedar sunburnt
paintbrush flame within her fingers on

the highway new-born lambs sleek chestnut
horse a trailer scoured pots and skillet flush

across the tree a nail. Each heart hungers
just for one.

Skid

The color flees the rabbits
flee this grind screech truck
braking steep-pitched ski jump
road, over

an accidental village

to which I can't return, reopen
like a badly broken leg, reset
the clock, remove 200,000 miles, rebuild
the metal joints, pierced bushings,
bent pins and torsion bars
that hold this mesh-work

its dual-carburetion, new
from the factory, the housings
with their warranties, painted
in our watercolors like an empire of clothing

waiting for embarrassment
the way a child's revelation
blows apart a wall of bricks,
as if some wolf

had taken you by huffing, puffing
until pages of our story turned from force of

Breath. Its dissipate spray. Indifferent spit. Spent

in months of combing your hair, tying
your sash just so. A knife under these fingernails,
prying for gray, black, the earth tones of clay

as if your voice were in the rust, a box
of greasy tools, gutted rags, two tons
of sliding screws and wheels

My foot jammed to the floor.

The Line

Step softly. This is the inn
where the line stopped. The deer
scatter. The rooms built of sound
hollow as guitars, bass violins, oaken
drums of whiskey. A candle's blot of punctuation

spread out on a table. The Finns
have left their mark here. The carvings
reek of caribou, punctured shapes. Boats
gliding through fiords. The chiseled runes

are Danes—dents of hammered words
angular and broken, a speech
their women could not deepen,
only pile, stone by stone, the womb
split by stone
giving birth to stone.

The beds, as well, were cairns. Here:
with both your hands—feel
these gouges, splintered even now
by chert and concretions. These
were my parents. Where they slept. Came

as you might come
into this chamber. The old man, his oilskin shoes, the
wife who took him on this floor, beneath her

coarse hair cloak. Took him like a cat. The rips, clawed
across the grain, are not imagination. Sit

with me, where he wades, boots
pulled up his thighs. His creel thick
with fish. Listen

to the graylings, each one cast ashore
drying block by block, dense as sides of salted beef, ships
stacked with slaves, hogsheads of molasses, fevered mares
bloated beyond ritual. Draw

your thumb along this scar: the hoof-prints
are there. The stream
barely a whisper. The road? Erased, but for a blur
running through the pine—back, forth—coursing
in the wood. Its dark, low pitch

the moan of a cougar.

Ana's Lamb

Alonso knocked. *The saw,*
I need the saw. Held

the bone-saw

by the blade, both hands
pale, as ripped as Easter.

Ana's lamb. In the pen—
the pen, the fucking pen.

A stock tank, stove-in,
strapped onto his pick-up. One

fender, hanging by rust. How
the moon was. Ana's lamb.

In the pen. The fucking *pen.*

Elope

Some pictures stay. The slip my daughter wears. *Look,*
my wedding dress. Her long dark sigh. The painter's
wooden ladder. A long dark stretch from window
to this road. For years the rungs climb up; an instant's
downward slide: scarves, combs, a mirror, the couple
finally breaking into moonlight and then gone. None

Of this today on the vacant rubbled causeway
that sluices from the mines. My father left this, as
his father did. As you will soon: your train whistling
behind. We wait along the tracks, all here do—blankets,
geese, sacks of salt and sugar, the crumbling haciendas,
stunted rows of thorn trees outlined by the frost. No

Winter comes to Pozos or the Balsas River that
does not wear a veil. Or the woven labor that shrouds
a man in sloughs, chopping lignite, the deep
crosshatches that mark a closing door. So we mark
ourselves. As road splits the village, the ladder pulls
the wall. As you draw your future from a hidden room.

In the stories of Matthew, the burro always awaits.
The burro has come. And kneels bridled at the steps,
with a bundle wrapped in cloth. The bones are the body.
The wood is the soul. The fire can happen. Now

Go strike your match.

The Most Handsome Man in America
—from a photograph, Northampton, Mass.

We see the bottom of a car, parked
at the top. A Packard, I'd guess. His family
drove Packards. Though this one's Brooks',
his roommate's. He'll return it tomorrow.

But the woman, stretched out on the lawn,
her head in his knees, eyes closed, looking up—
she'll stay. She's dreaming right now (you
know by her smile) of something that really

will happen. Or never took place. Because

of the war, she told me once, in Denver,
on the couch, her voice like bottled oxygen,
lying like this once again. But not
in this lush grass. Not with my father's hand

cradling her shoulder. Then, it's 1940.
They're both in school. He's driven for hours
to see her. The Germans, already, have taken
France. But nothing

invades them here. It's a fall day—you can
tell from the leaves, glistening, the soft
warm light that swims on the wheels, the
breeze in their face. And the hint of glass

where he lifts a bottle—round, milk punch,
to his mouth. How, she dreams (with her
own can of beer, clasped in both hands
over her heart), how *he'll* lift *her.* Before

the war. Tonight.

The Annunciation of Noah

—after a photo by Hiram Bingham, "Doorway, Machu Pichu," 1914

First I rose, hoisted you. That's what it was
to be a wall. Then I opened, crouched. That's
what it took to be a gate. Some women
get it easy: *down*—the body shoots. But you

stood back, half in, half out; your
thong-treads, frond-stripes, manta
open at the V, braced against decision
the way a reason does. I yelled, *Come on! Crows*

fly free! Car parts in the weeds, the roof's
caved-in, radios and furniture from one fence
to the other. I raked it, swept it, stirred, *Hey*
you! I took the tree and shook—*What*

have you to announce! The drummers hunched
on the wide earth bench and pounded. And
the hornplayers drank the corn-beer, and blew
the headlights wild. The Mennonites and priests

drove in from San Ixtápa, eyes blurred with candles, hands
with prayer and cheese. The dancers from the nightclub
wailed parrots, seethed *La Bamba*, churned
the jungle lizards—They broke the ox-beast's heart

and the ox-beast broke the bus. And the youth who
sells milagros unpinned his cape, flared out in silver—*Look*

here, we're all stars! Old Sandro with the gearshifts, curb-
side by the tavern, broke his little platform; got up

on both stubs, slugged the wheels at tourists. Then Sister
Magdalena, full of wings and sap, yelled, *I'm pregnant!*—
and threw up in the fire—*What's in a name, but who's
returned! Who are you but echoes, rock!* She

squatted in the rat-vines, on the backseat of a Ford.
From high across the ridge,

the waves began to roll.

Waving at People in Trucks

Look! Here's one now
ahead of mine, loaded
like a box-cart, hay bales
rumbling down a highway, body
through earth's body swerving
with these piñon trees splots of
sage excrescent aromatic dirt cow-spotted
hills, waving squeaking four-tire polished
blue sky-green Toyota mud just splattered
mud that's all that's running slick inside
the glass the lovers kissing thick
around a gearshift mud
the rocks, rot, dung and cactus dirt
with bales of hay the bursting
wires and here
her hand the wheel, can, cigarette, window
open free-blush girl with nothing
on but open highway open
fate-line life-line mound
of Venus oh
God how you spread

It's This That I Remember

How my friend sat at her table, hands
around her cup—both thumbs on the handle, air
sown with south-flying geese, the leather
chairs in languages

that squirrels know, trees know, all their
branches hesitant, listening
like a cloth, a skin that she might
sit within, or be astride, or wrap about her—

this cup, humid and brown, open
as the milkweed pods
fallen near the upper ditch,
that spilled out on the pasture

over the garden, into the broomcorn
and cabbage, dill-fans gone to seed,
the turning field of chiles
deep in their orange syllables, how

it was with the horses, and the money,
and the horses, and her youngest, now
at home instead of school, and
the horses, and her marriage,

and this slowness in her body, beyond
the slender photographs, the clean

tiles of the floor, the tablecloth
adjusted to drape evenly

over the dog—fat, sleeping
at her feet—and the horses,
and the bears who came each night,
rooted in the garden, rutted

in the pasture, drank, moaned,
screamed her name.

Field Trip

The kind of mirage my father would chip with his hammer
saying "See this rock" while it opened like a canoe, a skillet
drifting over a campfire, pebbled beans
sinking in red syrup, an occasional chunk of fat—

It makes little difference to the placing of the chairs, their straight
spines inherited from three generations of mytholithic upright
plantation-owners, ship-builders, stamped somehow
in every walnut leg, each apple stud, buried in the arm-rests, our wrists

"Floating" he'd say, poking with a spoon. This how the rations were—
Sicily, Normandy, Oran: oily abstractions known only by description.
Called our tanks "sardine tins," the Germans—Rommel
scared us shitless, mud-like, just drafted, a war we heard on radio—

Nothing talked about at supper, the entire Pacific Fleet, my mother stewing
Boiled New England Dinner in a five-quart Presto pressure cooker. Milk
in glass bottles, left on the porch, pasteurized, sealed with cardboard circles,
ribbed paper gussets, each one tied with

Words like clean, austere, utilitarian: perfect
for drill presses, certain kinds of knives, aluminum castings

But not for eating on the floor, the hacked tiles, for
hunkering beside this river. Its roar of spray, running salmon—
then the U-boats splitting water.

Tusas

Two trucks two trailers horse, saddled
in each one. The drivers sprawled, plastic
chairs, Tony's store for beans, tortillas,
mostly beer in twelve-pack *botes*
open on the counter. Tony, now
at almost eighty, back-hoe
parked behind the propane, speaks to me
in Spanish, them in English, though they
come from Michoacán—Juan, his brother Carlo,
just to herd the sheep. Tony's
sold the sheep, last year, a ranch
in Colorado; but, he's still got cows—Those
sneaky *vacas*—eight or maybe ninety, who
can tell; they're just that sneaky, hiding
on the Tusas up above Portrero—Boys
we need to find 'em. Every day

they don't.

Scout

So I'm looking at this thing—let's
call it a bear. Let's call it the soul. *Let's
call it*, we were calling in our red

caps with the fleurs-de-lis, up
against the line, our khaki shirts, green-
forest shorts, our blue, blue scarves,

we were up against a line that wouldn't
back down, between two trees in front
of the tent with somebody's hands, most

of the hands gripped to the poles
as if to hold it up, the soul I mean, the
shaking in the body just across

the twine stretched there
in the twigs on the dirt and the bodies
of the insects, a smell of grease and

shovels shoveling down a fog with its
sheet of superstition, clothes hanging up
and I'm wanting them back

because I'm right here
where it's rising like a bear, huge gaping
mouth, sharp gruesome teeth,

but I don't have a hat, some pants
more like pajamas, my scarf disappeared
before the orientation—and there's

no room left to grip, it's
a four-man tent, for their hands only—It's
a fact my shoes are loose and I've got

a bloodshot eye; the other one's floating
off to the left, up into the orbit
so I'm staring at this bear

and I'm looking direct, nothing in my fingers
dripping to the fog and it's got
some things to say—something like

a scream, more like a groan—just beyond
the line where it's more than wretched,
lifting its paws in the searchlight

of a throat with its red grieving horror and
the green snake teeth and the blue
thought of fear that everyone has left

with the pocket guide to slipknots, they've
taken the flashlights, jackknives, the matches
and the dice. It knows I'm alone. It knows

like a planet: Oh, I'm *ugly*. It knows
like Saturn. So I step across. It
knows I'm screwed. But it's got my eye

and I need to see.

Cows in a Field Outside El Rito

They don't move. Not today in hazy light,
May wind: a letter just torn open, an aging
body wrenching inside yours. They couldn't
care less. They don't. It's a modern day

in a modern year of bombing, price hikes, terror
pushed against its wall. Where wire, taut,
spikes and drives a fence: they notice—it
splits their grass from the alfalfa, greener, tall,
kept outside; but . . . who could care. Today

they're still. Hunkered down. With nestled
calves and rust-rot stumps, a pond, some cliffs,
a view of mountain snow. A cow
won't write like this. Only a son in a car,
stopped, dead still. Watching

the breeze, like brilliant glass, ripple
through a tree. Watching a child reach for a fork,
as turkey on its Christmas platter steams
into a room. It's a big space, Christmas—May,
April—all the mind can roam. And they

don't care. The fence is wired electric, strung
as far as Canada—as far as the eye conceives. No
eye sees the whole of *them*, one behind another,
rows of rock and motionless. Until you feel
the wind, pushing from within. Until you feel

a man, whose halting pen has pressed once
more: You could use this when you come. Get
some gas, a meal or two, a place to sleep on the
highway home. I need you to put up the star.
Your sisters will love to see you.

It's late spring. And the legs of the bull
are tucked, useless for now, beneath him. The
calves sunk in their mother's sides, eyes half-
closed in a dream of snow. We know
it's snow, all of us. And we know

it's about to fall.

The Welling

I did not invent this—no matter
how you read the red-smeared planks, nailed
like crooked fingers
to the gate's iced posts. Oak
splits from too much pressure, even
sunk that deep, the earth around
rammed as hard as cobalt. You remember
how the men—the plumber Almercer,
his sons Luis, Valente—the two who
share one brain, they say at Peña's store—
how they stumbled in from haying,
faces burnt, a fire of *Presidente*—took
the bar and shovel pressed
against the cages, took
off their shirts, took
that first breath. You remember
Clara's breath, fractured
by the cold; her bare arms, the open
sacks of gravel. She hated
the gravel. For two grains of freedom
I'd dump the gravel. Dump it
like a crude music. Dump it
in the stock pond, where
no weight is required. What
do fish care for traction? What
would a child say, staring
at ripples? The song
is not a mute inscription, a gesture

without motion. But something driven,
the way this truck writes road, two feet
compose a path—a spreading sound
marked by small round rocks
dropping. Dropping
while the plumber Almercer, his sons
lift a grey steel block
and set it on the flatbed. All
for the baling they say, all for sinking
two oak poles in a mass of limestone. All
for screwing through, a chain
between two limbs
to keep the music from advancing—as if
a fish would hear
the words in Clara's eyes, her torn
blouse, the thin clouds
moving away, silent from November.

Coal Seam

I'm out, the night again. The field. New growth
over September. Some black straw. Some burnt wheat.
Strange sun in a glass-fire.

Olivia was here. No cuts she said, it was your sweater. You
never knew how leaves could smolder. Never broke a slag-heap

for timbers in this cabin. No one asks, weren't they green—
I chinked them, who would care? I've touched

your back more than once. Held the earth
more than that—No cuts around the shoulders, only

what the mule felt, how the heavy tires
press a ton of steel, weights on either end—*A dumbbell's dream*

she said, two clean grooves, two stinking pits, two
lines of blood I'd smear the grass without you—I've counted

every blade, the way the trees went down, how
the mud took fire, two times three times four, the sheep
against the walls, the wool, the big Merino

walking by itself, walking out the lines, flaming
like the cry of God—*two times three times four*

Plein-Air, in a Palette of Eclipse

The shadow
holds our shape, two stones
on a crumbling fence of weather, canvas
pressed to a sea-blown table, wind
hissing in the trees. A white-gas lantern
trowels its plaster over splintered wood. Even

at noon, we feel the whir of owls, nighthawks
ghosting through a spent barn, smell hay
molding in the winter rafters. Pull
tufts of wool, last year's shearing, from
wire splayed around us. Yet the sky

still wheels its low lamped clouds, coastal
scenes of Holland: a landscape
made for sheep and children, sailboats
built from a corral, some corrugated tin,
the rolling drums of horses running, water
falling over Brittany—

where Gauguin, Monet, easels and umbrellas,
their women wrapped in cloth-like wings,

sit with us. A gray beach. Some random
spots you might call color. Brush-strokes hardly
different from the off-shore breeze
of dampened fires, distant cattle, churning

the relentless surf, dragging
ketches up the gravel. The paint

chips into layers: a laminate of mist, then smoke
that haunt its own opacity. No piano. No
guitar. Only the rain our daughter blows,
birds across a bottle of fog.

Puzzle

A sweetness, she says, strange now
how the air tastes, in these wharf-

shapes that form the room. Like sugar
into water, for the spinning birds, a kind

of sticky pink and then the ocean, gray
again, they alternate. Like boxes—waves

of boxes, the black and then the white,
each one lisping *Give a color, just a sound,*

the one that goes across—

Her table, with its lozenge tray, sea-green
pills. A silent glass of water, that

never will be emptied. She drops her pencil
in my hand. Canoe, she says, eleven letters—

canoe, *maroon canoe...*

When the Rockies Held the West

The Rocks' first year, one of the first games. I drove
north to Denver, met Dad at the house. My mother
had just died. It was Pittsburgh, Coors Field.
The seizures and the oxygen, all then months to come.
Dad took his Voyager. We parked at the Larimer lot.
He walked, slow but fine. He'd yet, with the maul, to shatter
his left foot. We hiked up to the thirteenth tier—perfect seats,
right above third base. Got hot dogs, extra mustard. Dad
corralled a Coke, I waved down a beer. Pittsburgh
muffed a steal, no score in its first. Then Eric Young, hot,
led off, connected *big—Home Run! Home Run!* After
that the game got tight. The Pirates snuck ahead. I got
Dad another Coke, myself another beer. Colorado
rallied in the sixth, bunted a run to tie. Dad started
singing, a song from college, I think. Then he began
to sob. In the ninth, Dante Bischette, just off the DL, with
Young on third, Girardi on first—Dante smacked a triple,
blew the game lights-out. The fans were on their feet,
cheering, throwing popcorn, programs, hats, scarves,
whatever they could find. Dad was hunched in his seat,
his face in his arms, a deep, convulsive moan welling
from his chest. I heard my mother's voice. Then
a horrid howl—like stricken wire, or a fuselage
over Hamburg, hit, splitting apart. *Dad!* I screamed—*Dad,
We've Got to Go!* I grabbed his palsied hand. I couldn't
find our shoes.

Sunset in Reno

No clouds, but *smoke*—the forest's on fire
beyond the sun behind the Nugget above

the rail that runs around this Motel 6. Outside
the concrete passageway, there's the below—

an all-night Arco lighting up
the billboards, neon, rolling dice, *Free* Cash

Coupon *Best*—Value *Best*—Payback *Two*
parents with their crippled son, stopped, between

their own and this room, staring at the all-at-once
illuminated steaks, strips of cars and streets, signals

blinking *Rock* puce *Rock* red *Hot* screen-
laser with its flashing streaks, bursts, *Stardust*, airline

blipping overhead—all for Elvis, for bombers
dumping slurry, for a mountain gone to flame, for

a slot machine's chance that one kid might walk, for
God's sake—*Mom, Dad, Look, the Stars!*

The Urgency of a Word Crossing into What Has Fallen

Has fallen from my mouth the Father says. He has an axe
which he calls a question. The question is decisive—

there are no small assertions. It crosses what the pain is.
A terror that's no animal's. Who freezes at your movement

when the tree pins the body. The Father and Son are crossing.
The terror is which one. The body on the tree, on the bank

of the road. Split by a wheel beneath the transmission. So
similar to wood the green comes automatic, the saturated

red. The man of flowers, outstretched like a child, thrown
from a story. Sharp as the teeth of a saw. As far as the act

of embrace.

Chainsaw

Just July, and my chainsaw's
in the truck.
A small model.
I bought it from Ingrid,
in the trailer up the road.
Her husband left it
when he left her, when
they'd spent her father's money—
Swedish things, a lot.
He took the Volvo and the rifles,
drove back to North Dakota
(he still coaches there).
Ingrid's blond. And short. The
saw's a Jonsered.
I got it for a song—some plastic
parts were broken. The bar's
hardly a foot.
But good for trimming
limbs. And oak.
Oak's the hottest:
not much girth, but clean, dense,
no splitting involved—

My stove's a Bergström, after all,
and I can't lift much
since the accident.

El Rito Motor and Limb

—for Kenny Coloden, Betsy Morrison

Kenny knows machines. Ignitions,
jeeps, chainsaws. Chairlifts, gears,
brakes, cables, things he learned in Aspen
off of Ruthie's Run. Today six cars,
my pickup and the twelve-volt
Coleman in his desert barnlot, scattered
stacks of straw and plastic, planking,
cross-lopped branches, bearings, fenders,
housings, oars, awls, loose
spools of fencewire since the landlord
pastures horses, just ninety bucks
a month, no water but electric
going on eight years, wood-heat, four
limping dogs from accidents, Betsy's
nursework brought them in. Kenny's
just off Interferon and the pilot program,
lucky, listen, lucky since they paid you
but now it's just small engines, fucked-up
cars and tree-trims suck, but look: He's
got land in Wisconsin. He's moving
back to Ashland, soon, soon as money
moves these part repairs, the big job
truck, the gasket set, hoses, timing
chain, flex-UV seals, new wiper shunts,
the burnt fan-clutch. *Soon* now plus
the overhaul, his blue Impala's motor.
Some rat chewed off the Coleman's starter,
stuffed rag strips up the air-filter, catfood

in the element, we knew the rivets
had to be replaced. He's finally
got the heater core to hook-up in his
Chevy with the re-bored stock three-forty
though we've got to *Floor It*—*Abbie! You
Brain-dead Abbie!*—Three-leg barking Sheltie
tearing through the pasture, landlord's crazed colt
stampeding through the crossgate—*Get Out, Abbie!*—
into paint-racks, fenceposts, pokeboat, broken
relays, rebuilt Carters, crashing push-rods,
pumps, bolts, throttles, gaskets dustflopped,
pistons ruined—*Screw you, Collie bitch!*
When he mounts that V-8 back . . . When
he mounts that V-8 back . . . *Oh* . . .
Abbie . . . !

Wood

Tony's about to go. Tony's
about to go. And now
he's brought me wood. And Brian,
who at thirty-five drives the truck
and stacks it full and
stacks it here again with me

for what, a thousand bucks
a month, that's seven days a week, to pay
his rent to Tony for two daughters who've
been sick, his pregnant wife, the meat
and beans from Tony's store the
beer the beer the
cases cases much now Brian
says too much its hard to save
for gas the car to always work but

Tony's about to go. And the old
man's brought me pine, he's brought
the clean pitch cedar, aspen
for the chimney red
potatoes cheaper than in Center
sweeter and just fist-size plus a six
of Red Hook Christmas Ale, today

Tony has a gift. And I have bucks
for him, worth all the vegetables

that never came
this summer when the beetles
killed the trees, rings of choking
borers when the drought
was at its worst. Tony

still works the counter
though he stands much harder
if at all still seven hours a day
since they cut his colon, found
the liver tumor—I wish

to tell you Tony that I
just talked with the *papas* and the brindle
she-goat that chews the Ford's upholstery
through the trashed-out window
of the year I was with Juana
in the deep ruts of the pasture
sloppy mud-wet with your daughter
watching the gray Paso mare, watch

the horse as she runs now, back
across the fields, back
arched running here again, again
the picture cannot hold her
or the fence that once was driven
pole to pole to nail to wire

the wish of grasses and
the freedom: Tony

is about. Tony is about, they say,
he tries like rock to claim itself
beyond the ditch, to raise up stumps
destroyed by fire, put back
water in the hole, Tony tries and

Brian tries since Tony works him
like a mule—Brian stacks, holds
his back, holds it back
because he has at least a job
for canned goods and a driveshaft
but also for the beer the smoke
the powder and the needle; God
knows how long that Tony's
got; now Brian's about
to go.

Motel Diana

The walls: thin. Thin
as the vision. The doors: flat
metal. Television
cars honk in the next room. A
woman, slapped, screams. This
is the story: the story of air. Air

in every room now, hissing
from its lines; while the vision
limps slowly, carved black cane,
drip in the shower, a roof
that will not shovel. The pain

is in the joists. The joints
twist, straining. And the TV knobs
turn up the language of blood. While
birds circle the fan jets, sucked
by the current. They

beat against the vents. We're waiting

for spring. We're waiting
for the manager, the blankets, the man
who lights the pilot. While the Grumman
turns slowly

in a World War movie, rolls away
with the gunners, and the oxygen,
turns from its squadron
and heads down to the target. Someone

in the parking lot
slams into a dumpster. Low in the back
where the fear is stalking. One hard
wheeze, cane-tap at a time. And I
face a blackened window—as my mother
once did, as my father does now

in a border-town motel, feeling the blood
punch into a wall, the screaming
down low. If I could find the knob. If
I could turn the hand, slide
the glass—*Hear them in there!*—Could

pull out the nails.

Alternative Power

How things work for me this autumn
since Red Dog's down by cancer,
my bursitis then the loneliness
for Farah driving County Twelve,
caliche rotten asphalt wrecked
both tie-rod ends the pinion rack,
with Buford in the housing
who can fix the blader. All of us
not home so much, Ed Taylor's
took three heart attacks last
Saturday was grisly. Still he talks
computers like a genius eats
his enchilada spills a bit
on how to print the photographs, he'd
do my book he says except
he's been pre-occupied; Epsons run
on batteries for
Lord's sake so can you.

El Niño

Welcome: my house, viewed from a plane.
Or helicopter. Or a statistic. If
you are uncertain, please come in.

As you see, the chimney
feels nothing like *Noche Buena,* forgive us
that leaving the stove

is impossible without assistance—
though two sparrows, a fledgling owl
are with you, all black. Through

the door, its window

a pile of wood, stacked against logs, crates
of crumpled paper, a box
of Fire Chief matches. My lover's clothes, scattered

chairs, thread on the floor, on the stairs

some silk. In the loft, the canvas
we are stretching, the glue sizing; on the table

plates, made by a woman
who talks with difficulty, turns slowly, the clay
like her intentions. The meal, simple:

timbales, squid, flattened with
an elbow, spice from China, rice in folded
envelopes, a fingerbowl with petals, the wine

and then the underlayer: as fine as hair, dark
as skin between us—black and hot
as charcoal. Where we stop, you begin—

Here. Let me help you with the door.

This is my house seen from a rock.

The Question

is his shirt. The same shirt, short-sleeve, faded
gray-green stripes that set the bruises off. They

leave him in it. The nurses. Week after week. Or simply
put it on again. Hundreds of shirts, my father. Closets

and closets. I always had the hand-me-downs. Lands'
End, Oxfords. Tasteful. Button clasp. I gave them

all away. Threw them out. I couldn't stand
them in my drawer, stuffed in there, piled for years

with insect stains, rodent-chewn. All fine once, just *fine!*—
What can I answer my life, when it comes clear:

I didn't use them, I don't care. All I need
are flannels: frost by mid-September, brutal snow

through May. Who cares? I don't dress for galleries now.
I hardly paint. *Hardly*'s not the question. The fine-weave

linen on my easel: blank for eighteen months. Or more.
I lie about some things. It's not important. All he asks

is a shirt.

Intimate Physics, Infinite Hand
—for Ruth and Rosendo Fuquen

Gathered in the daybreak room
beside my easel, Ruth,
her constant scarf wrapped blue
down over her temples, Rosendo
brawny, one by one
holding up the bright-hued
pictures. Talking here all
three of us, Ruth now
without cigarettes, about perception
as a dream, how colors
transform fields of vision,
and the think tanks
that he works for. A thing is not
an entity, just two or three
dimensions, not temporal at all;
but seen as we define it, or
explore it as an *opening*—A thing
will *blossom* says Rosendo
beaming as he shifts each painted
monotype to catch the filtered light
that softly pours its Mexico
from the outer window, over
pink geranium, bougainvillea,
buildings steeped with vines and
brilliant lemon, avocado buses
spouting plumes of diesel. A distant

campesino cuts brush with a machete:
sharp, swift, deft, exact—the way
a surgeon Ruth's known well
clears cancer with his art.
On a naked rooftop, two lovers
practice theirs: *Body, body*—a
yearning thing within itself, deep
as it can saturate, vast as it can
wash you—the sky, its palm
fronds, blush hydrangea
climbing into mist. Ruth
tightens her scarf, speaks of her new
sculpture. She makes it, she says
to *explain*. Rosendo, I, our spread-
arm urgent fingers, point the *world*,
reshaping, possible—the one
we now are entering. Ruth
grins, pushes up her breasts, like
sun-drenched tangerines. And
cups them, to her men. As if
they were there.

Hand-Knit Sweater

Now I'm in the sweater. The
imaginary sweater. Now

I'm in. Two-fifty in advance,
more for extra colors. I want

those extra colors—the thin
blue lines, free emerald particles

that thread a burning
star. Flecks of brilliant soft

in our long dark again. Your
breath still languid, an elbow

on my ribs. Your breast
turned to a dream, my ear

draped with curls. I bought
the wool in skeins, hanging

from a peg. I bought it all

for Valentina—Valentina's
hands, Valentina

with your art. Valentina
with her price to make

the warmth alive. I asked them
Please, have Valentina call.

I'm waiting by the phone.

You're talking in your sleep.

Flyer

Again my painting turns above the bird, the scattered
brittle patches that make its body still resilient: Faint

pinks of shattered please; blue so give me wings, repair
this thought of lying prone, leaving lost, all the question
envelopes that wrap a child's beginning. So the breath

of a four-year-old swathes a winter window,
the hills around New Haven. And this is how it works,
the tissue that holds bones intact, your features

after strafe, flak, implanted foreign organs. Wounds
speak, through scars' insistent vagueness: Reveal
me, enter me, you're not my losing act of ignorance.

Still I awake in the dark, hearing a sick
thud, sudden, into glass. Into sleet. Into the fog
of a child's desire. And now you lie, outside

the first year wings were broken, earlier than
Hiroshima, or the Flexible, or the iced-up runners

of the sled. You, on top, strong hands on mine
skidding steep, into inchoate vision, mound after
mound of spitting snow, spewing fracture, my split hold

shrinking underneath, into the wreckage of elms,
fields, a bird blanketed by ice, an oil-limned apparition
bowing down, as I pray here, over a haunted bed—

Outline us. Draw us, black, in the trees. Send us
back unfettered sky, your receding silhouette.

Treehouse

In this room: France. How the French
love their rivers! Raven
on a fencepost. Rhône. Say: *Rhône.*
Raven in cedars. Say: *fenêtre.* How
the French love their windows! Here
the shiny band, easels, Eiffel Tower. The
blue-line from Trieste, streaming
through Monet—where you *leapt,* I
lost my luggage . . . Who *cared*
about my luggage! I had wine (*lots*
of wine), a ticket home, an open plane
        no walls, no floor, a
        branch,
        you,
        a raven.

Still Life. With Bird

Perhaps I'm leaving tomorrow. Perhaps
the hotel's creaking gates
will open and shut one more time
beyond this afternoon. Beyond
this fountain still cascading
over the three-tiered pools, the bundle
of yellow roses—long-stemmed, wrapped
in plastic—left here at the edge
of a wedding; guests and mariachis
gone. Now it's mostly
empty, this restaurant, sliding
into shade. The gleaming
cars and trumpets, the flash-white
smiles of the bridesmaids,
departed. The gaping aunts and
sisters, bags of confetti, raucous
strings of cans; the laughter
of the uncles, lacquered with tequila:
elsewhere. The courage of the parents
beyond the trip, the bill, their wobbling
year's-wait legs; the bearded
ex-boyfriend, at the vows
bursting through the church
on a flame-red Kawasaki, taking
out a wall, the bride, the sixteenth-
century altar—all of this,

behind. Now, just burbling
water, the waiters, pacing
slow around the tables, and, in a cage
outside the kitchen, a canary—who,
with your glance, faintly warbles, jumps
through two blue loops, spins
a woven silver ball—until
you turn away
from the roses, the cresting
tropical trees, the re-announcing spill
of your singular life.

Flickers

When we begin like this, the earth turns to rain
and the rain begins to pour. Who
plays the drum? Who, across the roof, shakes
her tambourine? This month
up near the eaves, the topmost log, a family
of flickers
has made a pine-gum nest. Each night
I wake
to squawking, high-pitched squeaks. Wings
against the walls, stomping
on the tin. And now this tapping, sudden, down-
beats in the wood. My children, I think. My
beautiful. The stars blink
on their polar routes. The cabin
begins to shine.

Vinland

I say it is rain, for the rooster. And the fog,
and the dispersion of the small. And I say
it is rain for the sound of despair. For
the clutched breath in a child's dream
when the mare goes blind and licks
a wound. For the light I cannot reach. For
my father is building his boat.

And I say it is rain when it won't. For the sweat
in what is free. For deer as red
as the sorrow in wheat. A path cut through
a boy. For the map marked on a lover's thigh.
My father is building his boat.

I say it for the rooster, and the black bird leaving
his heart. For daybreak in a stairwell, still
finding its wings, the bread. For that first time
a girl comes wet. For the foal
that stands on its own. For that first time
the morning falls. My father is building his boat.

You'd say it's a song. It's not. My father
is building the rain—

Because the soul is permeable. I sit at this table
and cry. Because a woman
bleeds. I spread this floor and weep. Because

a man is mercury. My father is building: My
father. Because the child is water. I cup
these hands. I cup these hands.

So in the Infinite

moment when the music starts, the coffee
comes. A simple thing. Like silver
clacking in the sink, tap-water splashing
around a woman's hands. Perhaps
she's wearing gloves. Perhaps she's
wearing nothing. There are times
when a line goes naked; and we hear
a guitar. Or saxophone. Or
the pound of a hammer, in the distant
dark. A man building joists, a roof.
Setting a window
                    in a mud-work wall.

Araceli Chacón Draws a Picture of My Hand

—after a photograph by Hiram Bingham,
"Doorway, Machu Pichu," 1914

Inside the door the promised
is waiting. *Who?* Across a threshold desire is
calling. *Who?* You know he's the groom—or
is she the bride. Or the father's guitar; perhaps
a drum, slow-lobed, in a broad-striped blanket, straw
hat beneath the lintel. Or is this your mother,
crouched—hands, clawed, on her open knees
with *you* inside: a full-formed tongue,
pensive, resistant, hugging the frame
of rectangular speech. Or is this my *face*, shadowed
by roots over the eyes, nose sticking out
like a woman's nub, to turn around, or turn
below, that what was spoken was often a lie, that
here we lie, that this is a ruin, Peru, the head projects
as the gate of a room, that we go back, that we
come forth from breakage—limbs, twigs, the floor
of a stable, base of the jungle, the member up, announced
or come for a she who awaits, unshown,
her foreground like the looming background
the picture hides yet beckons from. No one's
in a room or a reed-mat bed that isn't there. The roof's
collapsed, the walls branch toward a viewpoint
and spread beyond, behind it. But this is an interior,
as speech is. And it knows the body, as she does,
the way her tongue knows yours.

The Adoption

Cesúly Guatemala beans and
the highchair. Can *stand*
in the highchair spoons forks plates
on the floor, fingers in the
beans Barbara's fingers
in the beans, Barbara's own slight
breasts, own small slender
Hold Cesúly *Hold* me—*Drop*
the tray the chair, weaving like
a loom its string its warps and w*ho's*
this dog? stuffed on top the enchiladas
in the chiles *Hot Cesúly Hot!* she says:
I couldn't take the blankets, tapestries, all
my weavings were for walls, floors, single
bodies in a bed, princess and the pea
the layers of onion wrapping
onion wrapping seed *only seed* beyond
the men who never could *they*
never could—but *there,* Antigua, *there*
this child Cesúly, harlequin, gypsy
hair, blouse, stars, diamonds
on her mother's hands, from the bed,
when she pressed her up to *me*: *Hold*
her darling Barbara, *Hold* her—*Drop*
the tray, *drop* the spoon—*Dear one,*
Spill your milk!

Peterbilt

So he falls again. And again. From the bed, the
stairs, his low-slung chair, my father, from my fable. As
night falls, I fall, as snow falls on the cabin, on routes
these years have cut in rock, the clutch, the scar
that wraps his forearm tighter to the wheel, turning
asphalt into dawn or dusk, the darkness
of a certain skin whose yearning spreads like fire. He's
driving wind now pressed against each stud, each
bolt and rivet in the gray ravines above the Mancos
pounding slate and rotten schist, sunken willow,
driving up the banks, the piling vaults, packing
freight in sleet, in seeking rain, each light
obscured by flesh, the red star route of backrow
streets, the black side-roll through Hatch, he's
driving grease the spitfire pots
the dirty coffee counter smears of more or don't
until the gears heat harder, higher up the Cumbres passage
into pine and sheet-bent poplar breaking back
beyond the throat of gasoline through grinding valves the glassy
skin near sudden bone of stare through father driving
blood twelve tons of sheep four tiers of panic bleating
shit my father drive me drive this son I push
against this stench the speed the gun-gray bales, against this box
behind the cab, the bed behind us farther farther throttled
beachhead splitcraft pylons crumbling steeper metal twisted
hands her face above the silos, fields, roast-pit red, pushed
to pavement, pistons, driving snow, driving bridge, the diving
likeness of yourself when the child came down in the mist of names.

Bamboo

There is a lake in the suffering. And
the horses come to drink. Their despair

like light, streaking from the prairie
as before a storm. The mare and her foal—

one larger in her balance, the other
spindly, legs as long as reeds. The song

is wind, then, water moving through bamboo,
the hollow of this grove of trees that speaks

where you might speak, straw and russet
candlelight—*Lie thee down, feathered child*

this is how the blanket sings, shuttled
on the loom, two threads of *in us do not part*

the open shell, deeper sorrow, the other
rawer, cutting anger, bracing here against

a promise. That you will be covered, and
rise up, like two with their necks, bent

down to this, milky, sucking—as I do now
for you, unsaddled, spreading, night.

Packet

A green light that comes
when you never saw it coming, never
heard it, felt it, but you *knew* it

like the woman in the sandlot
behind Abram's Grill
who's just lost her lenses,
on her hands and knees, her
hair cut short but seems as if
it's flowing, and the rush
on her throat like a rise
from birth, the music in the car

as the engine goes silent
while you fold down a seat
for the stashed beam lantern
with it's yellow plastic grip, six
Ray-O-Vacs, the
movement in the trees
beyond Lake Michigan. It's

a wave like that
when the wind gets lost
and the mail-boat from Racine, three
hours late, cracks into a tanker,
where the crew, like you, has
waited on the decks, in the hold
for two months out, to send

a message home—or to get a
certain scent, for just one instant,
of weeds, in the dirt, the both

of you groping.

Post-Partum

He's crying, and can't help it. The
fan's on, glasses clinking, customers

engaged in their talk. Not
with me. Not with you. You

hover—as you have
for now nine years—over

the tables, over his long extension
as he tosses in sleep, his hands

like an infant's: opening, closing,
reaching out for the one

who'll take him to her breast. Perhaps
he's me. Perhaps he isn't dead. But

waiting, as I am, for you
to pick him up.

Red Shoes

Today, Cinderella's hot: *Halláh!*— the red shoes
dance on amber. In the café on the tables *whip*

the omelet flambé ashes ashes cinder cloak
of dust to dash across the carpet chairs the ugly

rancher's sister's boots her leather face the straps
of black and silver swirling skirt below the bear

and elk heads stuck out ogle stiff their stuff dumb-
struck by pumping pumps these dashing arms

this buckling swash of air through silk the brewer's
art the ranger's jokes *Halláh!*— Cinderella's not

for watch our hands but sweep tall grasses in the
hula swish us vine-spice winter gusto mango waves

the sound of breakers rolling carriage midnight
noon to highway up the chimneys circle every

guest who comes to beat the spoons and forks
to clatter plates ceramic *ping* clear bells on toes smooth

valley cows the bucking goat in Carlos' pickup every
window open with the smokers mad health-workers

as the stove fires *Pow!* the kitchen flames for all
will know now after sizzle after steak the pumpkin

pie now comes the prince the clicking clock
the pigtails circling arms true inching straight up *crash*

the platters tumblers fresh-poured coffee gushing
out the door spring *up* the tailgate on the grain stack

white angora leaping Cinderella flying feedsacks star-
burst shower   *Halláh!*—   for the one that Carlos

                              carries home tonight!

Bringing in the Name

Now the graces gather
in the meadows near Petaca
above the Mesa Vista down
a crossroad's swollen
river where the hot springs
steam. My cousins
are in vapor with the youngest
here expecting
and the fluming shrub-oak
around Cornelia turn. Her
lips bright red so full
they lift each sister's shadow you
can hear our bluetick Aldo twenty
coyotes barking
as all dogs will do. When
a woman threads her water let
us sing into her belly every
cattail bursting
silky luff that floods the hayfields
with the tractor still in fescue
for a last September pick-up
on this golden freshness morning just-
dropped bales so
green and fragrant that I
call them out in buckgloves hay-
hooks Hanna's new-brewed coffee just
like children *Sara! Juan! Elena!* I
lift each one to God.

Fresas

—Café Las Monjas, San Miguel de Allende

The couple from Chile with the two-
year-old girl. What brings them here? Don't
ask *them*. Their daughter's

hitting melon with the edge of a spoon, soon
whacks a pineapple, sliced, into bits. Her parents
drawn together in their own exchange.

The woman's pregnant. Very pregnant. The most
beautifully pregnant I've ever seen. Her hair's
swept back—from her summer-summoned face,

her guava blossom lips, her green mango eyes—
it flowers from a topknot, tied with a bow, a geyser
of reed-grass spilling as she laughs. Her husband's

laughing too. He lofts a coffee pitcher
over his head, reaches out for her deep-curved cup.

The daughter creams a ripe banana on their Frommer's
guide. Thumps the handle of a knife, cracks the rim
of a plate; then rips a baked *bolillo* into seeded shreds.

His wife, gazing elsewhere, smoothes a floor-length scarf.
He smoothly butters the rest of the bread. His own hair's
tousled. Is he, perhaps, waiting for a sign? Suddenly

the daughter overturns her chair, vaults
onto the table, hugs her mother, wraps both parents

in the long red scarf. Then she hugs them both. *Fresas!*
she shrieks. Strawberries! Her father jumps up, throws
the scarf in the air. *Fresas!* he shouts, *Fresas Por Sí!*

And his wife screams, *Fresas!* The tables stomp, *Fresas!*
The whole restaurant howls, *Fresas!*—Until the mother glows
like a bright scarlet lamp, like strawberry wine,

the wide floor splattered with tumbling fruit.

Canticle for a Winter Mesa

This was the week
the snow began. Christmas
then tsunami, falling
trestles, flying jets
our legs touched
on the desert. The weak

pneumonia filled my lung, suddenly
left. In the oriental wood a hundred
pipes and flocking birds, feather
water deepest. Comfort me, bed,
comfort us. Two in
aloe and bells. Listen again

to the donkey. Listen
to hooves and the saw,
for the trumpets were first,
then the tambourines, the secret
rites of carpenter. This
was the gabled house

that opened its wish to
room for us. Take, take
our sorrow larger. Sound
of the wire, the brick
that hard nights mold. A thousand
notes of flame-built hope, our

vessel hold the fire. Let it rise
new vehicle—and spread
upon our waiting. For this
is the time of bear. The song
of the cloven tree, its rounds
now circling open. For those

who hold this ring. Who
hold this sacred. And snow,
the tap at the window, the
shoes. To put on
the stars. The sierras
are lit. Deep, on the porch:

Cover me.

Thanks and Acknowledgments

Grateful acknowledgment is made to the editors of the following publications in which these poems have appeared:

Beloit Poetry Journal, Best New Poets 2007 ("Peterbilt" selected by Natasha Trethewey), *Chariton Review, Comstock Review* ("Elope" chosen by Cornelius Eady for the 2005 M.C. Bailey Prize), *Del Sol Review, 5AM, Five Fingers Review, Hollins Critic, Lyric Review, Margie: The American Journal of Poetry, Marlboro Review, Northwest Review, Paris Review, Perihelion, Poetry East, Studio, Sulphur River Literary Review, Texas Review, Western Humanities Review.*

My infinite thanks to: Christine Hemp, her flute; Carolyn Forché, her guts; Cathy Strisik, her love of these songs & lambs forever; Lise Goett, 'Annah, Lisken VP Dus, Katie Kingston, Jenny Mac, who've shaped, given balm and tuning. Brigit Kelly, her heart and magic, bringing the flock into the oak. Barbara, Jennifer, every colleague from San Miguel, Ithaca East, Patzcuaro. Doug Scott, who's kept me off the ceiling. Martha Rhodes, all at Four Way Books who've let it fly. To every friend, my family—on every bus, in every rain, on every road and bridge.

Jamie Ross was born in Connecticut, grew up in Colorado. At the age of ten, he won a red Schwinn bicycle in a comic strip contest sponsored by the Denver Post. He's been writing, drawing and traveling ever since. A member of the first National Geographic Yukon expedition, he's lived in Iran, Italy, spends much time in Mexico, currently resides on a mesa west of Taos—where he chops wood, hauls water, and rebuilds his Toyota truck. His poetry was selected for the 2005 Muriel Craft Bailey Award, also included in the national anthology *Best New Poets 2007*.